Tsunami

Perspectives on tsunami disasters

Ian Graham

Raintree is an imprint of Capstone Global Library Limited, a company incorporated in England and Wales having its registered office at 7 Pilgrim Street, London, EC4V 6LB – Registered company number: 6695582

www.raintreepublishers.co.uk
myorders@raintreepublishers.co.uk

Edited by Andrew Farrow, James Benefield and Claire Throp
Designed by Philippa Jenkins
Original illustrations © Capstone Global Library Ltd 2014
Picture research by Tracy Cummins
Originated by Capstone Global Library Ltd
Printed in China

ISBN 978 1 406 28032 6 (hardback)
18 17 16 15 14
10 9 8 7 6 5 4 3 2 1

ISBN 978 1 406 28038 8 (paperback)
19 18 17 16 15
10 9 8 7 6 5 4 3 2 1

British Library Cataloguing in Publication Data
A full catalogue record for this book is available from the British Library.

Acknowledgements
We would like to thank the following for permission to reproduce photographs:
We would like to thank the following for permission to reproduce photographs:
Corbis pp. 4, 11 (© Mainichi Newspaper/AFLO/Nippon News), 12 (© DAMIR SAGOLJ/Reuters), 13, 23 (© Michael S. Yamashita/National Geographic Society), 21 (© Buddy Mays), 25 © Toru Hanai/Reuters), 44 (© POOL/Reuters), 45 (© Noboru Hashimoto); Getty Images pp. 14 (JIJI PRESS/AFP), 22 (YASUYOSHI CHIBA/AFP), 24 (MIKE CLARKE/AFP), 29 (YOSHIKAZU TSUNO/AFP), 30 (AFP), 31 (AFP PHOTO/KAZUHIRO NOGI), 33 (London Stereoscopic Company), 34 (BERTRAND LANGLOIS/AFP), 39 (Asahi Shimbun), 40 (NICHOLAS KAMM/AFP), 41 (Sankei), 42 (TOSHIFUMI KITAMURA/AFP), 43 (Christophe Licoppe/Photonews); Newscom p. 37 (Toru YAMANAKA); Science Source pp. 8, 9 (GeoEye); U.S. Air Force p. 26 (Airman 1st Class Katrina R. Menchaca); U.S. Coast Guard photo p. 20 (Petty Officer 2nd Class Brandon Thomas).

Cover photograph of waves swallowing a seaside village near the mouth of the Hei River, Miyako City, Japan, 11 March 2011, reproduced with permission of Corbis (© AFLO/Nippon News).

Disclaimer
All the internet addresses (URLs) given in this book were valid at the time of going to press. However, due to the dynamic nature of the internet, some addresses may have changed, or sites may have changed or ceased to exist since publication. While the author and publisher regret any inconvenience this may cause readers, no responsibility for any such changes can be accepted by either the author or the publisher.

Contents

Some words are printed in bold, **like this**. You can find out what they mean by looking in the glossary.

DOSSIER:
THE 2011 JAPANESE TSUNAMI

In 2011, a massive earthquake off the north-east coast of Japan triggered one of nature's most destructive events, a tsunami. A tsunami is a series of giant waves caused by an earthquake or other disturbance. The 2011 tsunami swept over the Japanese coast and continued inland. Whole towns were destroyed. Thousands of people died. Hundreds of thousands of buildings were swept away or damaged. Millions of homes were left without electricity or drinkable water. Nuclear power stations on the coast were damaged, one of them so badly that it caused one of the most serious nuclear accidents that has ever happened. The scale of the disaster faced by the Japanese people, government and rescue workers was enormous.

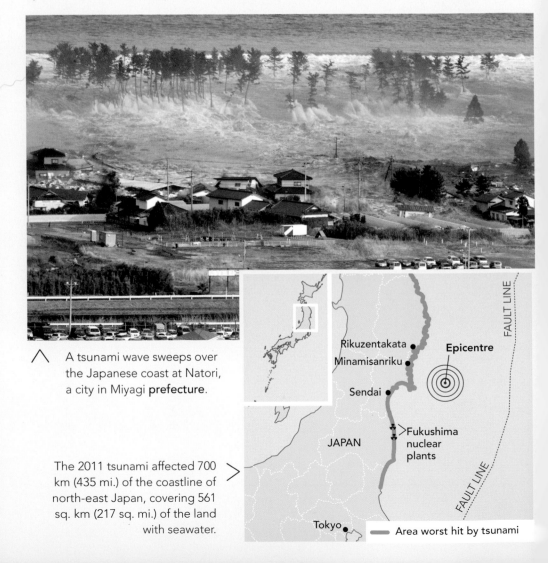

∧ A tsunami wave sweeps over the Japanese coast at Natori, a city in Miyagi **prefecture**.

The 2011 tsunami affected 700 km (435 mi.) of the coastline of north-east Japan, covering 561 sq. km (217 sq. mi.) of the land with seawater. >

Rikuzentakata •
Minamisanriku •
Epicentre

Sendai •

FAULT LINE

JAPAN

Fukushima nuclear plants

FAULT LINE

Tokyo •

━━ Area worst hit by tsunami

DATE:	11 March 2011
LOCATION:	north-east region of the island of Honshu
NUMBER OF RESIDENTS:	10 million
MAGNITUDE OF THE EARTHQUAKE:	9.0 on the moment magnitude scale
MAXIMUM HEIGHT OF THE TSUNAMI:	40.5 m (133 ft.) at Miyako City
HOW FAR INLAND THE TSUNAMI REACHED:	up to 10 km (6 mi.) at Sendai
CASUALTIES:	15,883 dead, 2,667 missing, 6,145 injured, 590,000 people evacuated
DAMAGE:	1.2 million buildings, 4.4 million left without electricity, 1.5 million without water
ESTIMATED COST:	25 trillion yen (£191 billion)

JAPANESE TSUNAMI TIMELINE

11 March, 14:46
A magnitude 9.0 earthquake occurs close to the north-east coast of Japan

14:48
Tremor felt in Tokyo

15:12
A 6.8-m (22-ft.) tsunami wave hits Iwate Kamaishi-oki

15:41
A 14-m (46-ft.) high tsunami wave sweeps over Fukushima Daiichi power station and puts its back-up generators out of action

15:44–15:55
More tsunami waves crash into the coast, reaching 7.3 m (24 ft.) high

19:30
The government declares a nuclear emergency

21:23
Residents within a 3-km (2-mi.) radius of the Fukushima nuclear power station are told to leave their homes

Killer waves

The 2011 Japanese tsunami was caused by an earthquake under the Pacific Ocean, near the coast of Japan. The main earthquake was preceded by powerful foreshocks and followed by hundreds of aftershocks. Tall buildings in Tokyo swayed violently. Roads cracked. A dam collapsed.

The ocean floor had suddenly jumped upwards along a crack in Earth's **crust** called a **fault line**. This lifted part of the ocean upwards. Water always flows downhill, so the huge bulge of water flowed away in all directions in a series of waves – a tsunami.

A tale of four plates

Japan suffers tsunamis because it straddles four massive **tectonic plates** (the plates of rock that Earth's crust is made of). They are the North American Plate, the Eurasian Plate, the Philippine Plate and the Pacific Plate. All the plates are moving very slowly. The Pacific and Philippine Plates are moving towards the Eurasian Plate and pushing it and the North American Plate in between down underneath it. This is called **subduction**. The edges of the Eurasian and North American Plates are dragged down until they jolt free and jump upwards, causing an earthquake. If the movement is big enough and fast enough, it sets off a tsunami.

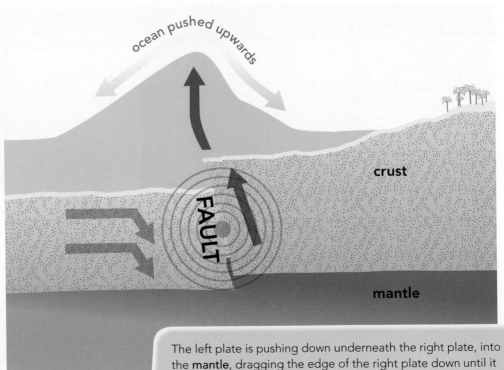

The left plate is pushing down underneath the right plate, into the **mantle**, dragging the edge of the right plate down until it eventually shakes free and bounces upwards. This raises the ocean above the fault and triggers a tsunami.

The part of Earth's crust that Japan sits on is criss-crossed with faults where immense plates of rock meet and push against one another.

NORTH
AMERICAN
PLATE

PACIFIC PLATE

EURASIAN
PLATE

PACIFIC
OCEAN

Sea of
Japan

•Tokyo

Direction of movement
Edges of plates

PHILIPPINE
PLATE

What causes tsunamis?

Earthquakes aren't the only events that can cause tsunamis. They can be caused by landslides. In 1998, a massive underwater landslide off the coast of Papua New Guinea caused a tsunami. Tsunamis can also be caused by a very rare cosmic event. A huge **comet** or **asteroid** smashing into an ocean from space would produce a giant tsunami.

TSUNAMIS THROUGH HISTORY TIMELINE

1600 BC, Santorini, an island in the Aegean Sea
Destroyed the Minoan civilization on Crete

1755, Lisbon, Portugal
Killed up to 40,000 in Portugal, perhaps 10,000 in Morocco and others as far away as Britain and Ireland

1771, Great Yaeyama tsunami, Japan
12,000 killed by a 30–85-m (99–279-ft.) high tsunami

1908, Messina, Italy
70,000+ dead

1958, Lituya Bay mega-tsunami, Alaska
Highest recorded tsunami in history – 524 m (1,740 ft.)

1976, Moro Gulf, Mindanao, Philippines
7,000+ dead

2004, Asian tsunami, Sumatra, Indonesia
Highest recorded deaths – 230,000 in 13 countries

2011, Tohoku tsunami, Japan
18,550 dead or missing after 40-m (130-ft.) high tsunami

Jet-speed waves

Tsunamis travel across an ocean incredibly quickly. They can move at up to 800 kilometres (500 miles) per hour – as fast as a jet airliner! When the earthquake on 11 March 2011 triggered a tsunami about 130 kilometres (80 miles) from Japan, it took less than 30 minutes for the first wave to hit the Japanese coast.

Out in the deep ocean, tsunamis are not very high, but their energy actually extends to the bottom of the ocean. As the tsunami waves approached the coast, they grew higher. This happened because the front of each wave was slowed down by friction with the increasingly shallow seabed. Water coming behind caught up with the front of the wave. The gathering water had nowhere to go but upwards, building a higher and higher wave.

Destructive power

The tsunami waves were so destructive because they were different from normal sea waves. Waves that wash onto the shore every day have a wavelength of a few metres. The tsunami waves that hit Japan had a wavelength of several kilometres. Each wave had the weight of several billion tonnes of water behind it. This forced the waves onto the shore and kept on pushing them inland.

Before (left) and after (right) photographs of the coastal town of Rikuzentakata show the devastating destruction caused by the tsunami.

The water forced its way up rivers and valleys. The height and power of the tsunami in different places depended on the shape of the coast and seabed. Residents more than 3 kilometres (1.9 miles) inland in Rikuzentakata thought they were safe, but the town was destroyed because its bay and river valley were the perfect shape to funnel the waves through it. The waves swept away everything in their path.

Mega-tsunamis

The biggest tsunamis are called mega-tsunamis. They can travel up to 25 km (15 mi.) inland. When a volcanic **avalanche** caused by the eruption of Mount St. Helens in the United States in 1980 surged into Spirit Lake, it caused a mega-tsunami 260 m (850 ft.) high. Some scientists think the Cumbre Vieja, a volcano in the Canary Islands, could split in two the next time it erupts, and part of it may fall into the Atlantic Ocean. It could generate a tsunami up to 1,000 m (3,300 ft.) high that would still be 30 m (100 ft.) high when it reached North America.

Meltdown!

As the tsunami approached Japan, the Fukushima Daiichi nuclear power station lay in its path. The power station was built on the coast because it needed a constant supply of water for its cooling system. It was designed to resist earthquakes and tsunamis, but the 2011 tsunami was so much bigger than the power station designers had planned for, and it overwhelmed the building's defences. The earthquake knocked out the station's main power supply, but there were back-up generators. However, the tsunami flooded the generators and put them out of action. Without electricity, the power station's cooling system failed and so the fuel in the **nuclear reactors** began to overheat. The cooling water in three of the reactors boiled away and the fuel heated up so much that it started to melt. This is called a **meltdown**.

A nuclear meltdown is very serious, because it is possible for the fuel to melt through the vessel containing it or for explosions to blow the reactor apart, releasing **radioactive** material into the environment. The severity of nuclear accidents is measured on an international scale that goes from 0 for the most minor accident to 7 for the most serious imaginable. There have been approximately 20 meltdowns in the thousands of nuclear reactors built since the 1950s, but only two level 7 accidents. One was the Chernobyl disaster in 1986, when a powerful explosion in a reactor in Ukraine spread radioactive fuel over a wide area. The other occurred at Fukushima Daiichi after the 2011 tsunami.

Inland tsunamis

One of the strangest tsunamis occurred in Italy in 1963 when a 250-m (820-ft.) high wall of water swept down the Piave Valley, killing 2,000 people. The valley was not on the coast. A dam had been built across it. People thought the dam must have collapsed, but it hadn't. A landslide had fallen into the **reservoir** behind the dam, pushing 50 million cubic metres of water over the dam and into the valley below.

DOSSIER:
FUKUSHIMA DAIICHI

Fukushima Daiichi is one of the world's biggest nuclear power stations. It was built in the late 1960s and early 1970s. Its six reactors are a type called a boiling water reactor because heat from **nuclear fuel** in the reactor boils water to make steam, which drives electricity generators. The steam is then cooled by water pumped in from outside the plant and changed back into water so that it can be sent through the reactors again. As a result of the 2011 earthquake and tsunami, three of the reactors were badly damaged and had to be shut down. The three remaining reactors were not operating at the time of the tsunami.

QUICK FACTS

NAME:	Fukushima Daiichi
LOCATION:	Ōkuma, Fukushima, Japan
BUILT:	1967–1971
NUMBER OF NUCLEAR REACTORS:	6
TYPE OF REACTORS:	boiling water reactors
POWER OUTPUT:	4,696 megawatts (enough to supply power to more than 4 million homes)
OPERATOR:	Tokyo Electric Power Company (TEPCO)
STATUS:	out of service because of tsunami damage

<

The Fukushima Daiichi nuclear power station received a direct hit from the giant 2011 tsunami, which put it out of action and badly damaged some of its reactors.

In the disaster zone

Japan is one of the best-prepared countries when it comes to tsunamis. The land and seabed are peppered with hundreds of instruments monitoring ground movements. One of the first signs that something serious had happened on 11 March 2011 came from Global Positioning System (GPS) instruments near the earthquake's **epicentre**. They accurately record their position using radio signals from satellites orbiting Earth. One of the instruments on the seabed suddenly shifted 4 metres (13 feet) sideways. The earthquake that did this also pushed part of the seabed 7 metres (23 feet) upwards. This upward movement produced the tsunami. Meanwhile, part of Japan's coastline dropped by 0.6 metres (2 feet), making it even easier for the tsunami waves to come ashore.

Tsunami evacuees are given food and shelter at an evacuation centre in Kesennuma.

Practising for disaster

Tsunami drills, rehearsals of what to do when a tsunami warning sounds, are routine in Japanese coastal towns and schools. Street signs mark out areas at risk and tell people to leave if a warning sounds. Tsunami drills saved many lives, because people knew what to do when the warning sounded.

Warnings are given

Scientists issued a serious tsunami warning in Japan, and to coastlines and islands elsewhere in the Pacific Ocean. As the waves spread across the ocean, **buoys** reported them passing and measured their height. The warnings in Japan were for a tsunami higher than 3 metres (10 feet), the most serious warning that could be issued, but the tsunami actually reached more than 40 metres (131 feet) in some places. This led to a slow evacuation, because people didn't know how bad the coming disaster would be.

How did people react?

Just over half of the people in the affected area immediately moved to higher ground or taller buildings. People didn't want to leave their homes, because they felt safe there, but, reluctantly, they left – they knew they had to escape.

This street sign in Minamisanriku warned people to leave if they heard a tsunami warning siren. The town was devastated by the 2011 tsunami.

False security

A 73-year-old man called Tsuyoshi Kinno remembered the town of Rikuzentakata being badly damaged by a tsunami in 1960. In 2011, when he saw dozens of people sheltering in the town's community centre, just a few hundred metres from the shore, he knew they were in danger. He urged them to get out and make for the top of the taller four-storey City Hall.

Apart from a handful of sturdy concrete buildings, the Japanese town of Minamisanriku and thousands of its citizens simply disappeared on 11 March 2011.

The people felt safe in their community centre and were reluctant to leave without official instructions to do so. Mr Kinno, with a different perspective gained from experience, begged them to leave. Only 15 or so of them made it to the top of the City Hall in time. The others died, swallowed by the tsunami's black water. Tsuyoshi said, "People relied too much on the order and **bureaucracy**. They became too obedient. In olden times, they would have just got straight to the mountains, to higher ground."

Nature's warning

One warning sign that a large tsunami is approaching the coast is the sight of the sea drawing back from the land and exposing the seabed. Just before the devastating Asian tsunami of 2004, people on the southern coast of Java saw the sea suddenly rush 450 m (1,500 ft.) away from the beach, leaving fish flopping about on the seabed. Some of the people knew this meant that a tsunami was coming and they fled from the beach to higher ground.

A roar in the distance

When the tsunami struck, English teacher Shinji Saki was teaching his class high up on a hill overlooking the town. He heard a roar in the distance and then saw the huge wave approaching the town. He estimated that about 7,000 people had made it out of the town onto the hill where he stood. More reached the hill on the opposite side of the town. The rest of the town's residents died because they didn't get out in time. Shinji said he saw a man floating away on **debris**, but there was nothing he could do to save him. That day, all the children were in school and all the schools were built high up on the hills. But their parents were at home and work, down in the valley. Many of them died, leaving thousands of children orphaned.

What would you do?

Imagine hearing a warning telling you to leave your home immediately. You don't know if you'll ever be able to go home again. What would you take with you on the way out of the door – family photographs, mobile phone, pet dog? You can't take everything. What would you choose?

Helpless

"We watched as our entire town was swept away. It just no longer exists."

Shinji Saki, a teacher in Minamisanriku

A nuclear crisis

Meanwhile, the attention of workers at the Fukushima Daiichi nuclear power station was on other events. They were trying to deal with the worsening crisis there. They couldn't get back-up generators working because of the damage caused by the tsunami. Without a working cooling system, they couldn't control rising temperatures inside the reactors. They let hydrogen gas escape from the reactors to reduce the pressure inside. Television pictures showed this gas exploding, blowing the buildings apart. Engineers eventually decided to pump seawater into the reactors to cool the fuel. Allowing impure, corrosive salty water in meant that the reactors could never be used again.

When the power company ordered the workers to stop, the plant manager, Masao Yoshida, did something almost unheard of in Japanese companies. He believed that the company's instruction was wrong and so he disobeyed orders and continued pumping in the seawater. His courage and independent thinking probably prevented an even worse disaster. Sadly Mr Yoshida died of cancer, said to be unconnected to the nuclear crisis, in 2013.

Four nuclear power stations in the region affected by the tsunami were shut down after the earthquake. Onagawa survived undamaged. Fukushima Daini and Tokai Daini were flooded but shut down safely. Only Fukushima Daiichi suffered severe damage and meltdown.

TIMELINE:
THE FUKUSHIMA DAIICHI POWER STATION

11 March, 11:14:46
The earthquake shakes the ground so violently that the electrical supply to the power station is cut off and the power plant shuts down automatically

15:27
The first tsunami wave arrives

15:35
A 14-m (46-ft.) high tsunami wave sweeps over the power plant's tsunami wall and puts the diesel-powered back-up generators out of action

19:03
A nuclear emergency is declared by the government

20:50
Residents living within 2 km (1.2 mi.) of the power station are evacuated

21:23
The evacuation order is extended to 3 km (1.9 mi.)

12 March, 05:30
Steam is released from one of the reactors to reduce the pressure inside

05:44
The evacuation order is extended to 10 km (6 miles)

10:58
Steam is released from a second reactor

15:40
An explosion rips one of the reactor buildings apart

18:25
The evacuation order is extended to 20 kilometres (12 miles)

20:20
Engineers start pumping seawater into the reactors to cool them down

Following days
There are further explosions in the power station, and workers continue pumping water into the damaged reactors and dumping water on them from helicopters to cool them down

Evacuation

The Japanese government ordered the evacuation of people living within 20 kilometres (12 miles) of the Fukushima Daiichi nuclear plant. The US Nuclear Regulatory Commission (NRC) took a different view. If the same event happened in the United States, they would evacuate everyone within 80 kilometres (50 miles) of the plant. On 17 March, the US Ambassador in Japan advised all Americans within 80 kilometres (50 miles) of the power plant to leave the area.

More than 300,000 people were evacuated. However, the evacuation ended up causing many more deaths than are likely to be caused by **radiation**. These included illnesses resulting from hospital closures, exhaustion caused by moving to evacuation centres, and even suicides caused by stress and fear. Although radiation caused no deaths, the possibility of radiation exposure still worried people. The discovery of raised radiation levels in drinking water as far away as Tokyo added to their fears.

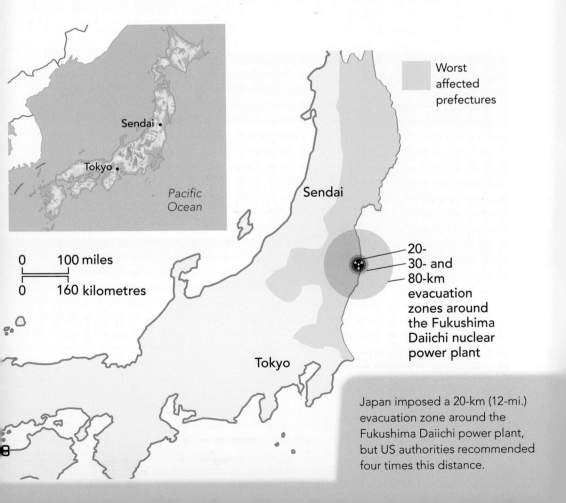

Worst affected prefectures

Sendai

Tokyo

Pacific Ocean

Sendai

Tokyo

0 — 100 miles

0 — 160 kilometres

20-
30- and
80-km evacuation zones around the Fukushima Daiichi nuclear power plant

Japan imposed a 20-km (12-mi.) evacuation zone around the Fukushima Daiichi power plant, but US authorities recommended four times this distance.

US fears

The prevailing winds from Japan blow east across the Pacific Ocean towards the United States. Despite reassurances from scientists, fears of wind-borne radioactive **fall-out** led to a run on potassium iodide tablets on the west coast of the United States. Potassium iodide blocks the body's uptake of radioactive iodine. However, only tiny amounts of radioactive fall-out reached the United States.

Nuclear attack

The Japanese people are particularly sensitive to news of radiation leaks. This is because Japan is the only country that has ever experienced nuclear attacks in wartime (in 1945) and has had to deal with large numbers of people suffering from radiation sickness. About 94,000 people survived nuclear attacks on two cities, Hiroshima and Nagasaki. Those who are still alive today, more than 65 years later, continue to be monitored and studied.

A nuclear emergency worker's story

On 24 March 2011, 13 days after the tsunami, a squad of workers entered the damaged Fukushima Daiichi reactor buildings. One of them, known only as Shinichi to hide his real identity, said the workers put on all-over protective clothing – hazmat (hazardous materials) suits, gloves, rubber boots, helmets and face masks. Each wore a **dosimeter**, a device that measured their radiation exposure.

They entered the Reactor 3 building through a hole in the wall because its electrically operated door was out of action. Beams of light from their helmet-mounted lamps cut through the darkness and revealed ankle-deep water on the floor. As they waded through it, it felt warm through their boots. Steam rose from it. Shinichi said, "If you're a nuclear plant worker, you know that water on the floor is bad news. You just don't touch it." One worker whose boots leaked suffered minor radiation burns. Mangled metalwork and rubble caused by explosions lay everywhere. The men had to take care not to trip up and fall into the radioactive water.

Another team of workers left quickly when they encountered a pocket of dangerously high radiation. Shinichi's team stayed to check the building's electrical systems and lay new power cables. Shinichi worked in the damaged, flooded and radioactive building for 13 days.

Further afield

The biggest tsunamis can cross an ocean and still have enough power to be dangerous. When an earthquake caused a tsunami near the Aleutian Islands in the northern Pacific Ocean in 1946, the tsunami crossed the ocean and killed 159 people when it hit the Hawaiian Islands 3,800 kilometres (2,360 miles) away. The Hawaiian Islands were hit again in 1960, when a tsunami off the coast of Chile crossed the ocean and killed 61 people. The 2011 Japanese tsunami caused casualties and damage as far away as California, USA, and Chile. It was just 2 metres (6 feet) high when it reached the Californian coast, but that was enough to wreck dozens of boats and wash away one man. Chile evacuated 700,000 people from coastal communities and closed its ports. When the tsunami arrived, it slammed fishing boats into docks, and some areas lost power and water supplies.

The 2011 tsunami washed millions of tonnes of debris off the land into the sea. Most of it sank immediately, but anything that floated was carried away by ocean currents. Some of it floated all the way across the ocean to the west coast of Canada and the United States.

The Japanese fishing boat *Ryou-Un Maru* burns after a US Coast Guard ship opens fire on it to sink it off the coast of Alaska.

This 18-m (60-ft.) long dock was one of the first pieces of debris from the 2011 Japanese tsunami to reach US shores when it washed up on a beach in Newport, Oregon, in 2012.

Ghost ships

Several boats washed out to sea by the tsunami were carried all the way across the Pacific Ocean. They took a year or more to make the journey. When these "ghost ships" were spotted off the coast of Canada or the United States, aircraft were sent out to check if anyone on board was alive. No survivors were found. The US Coast Guard sank one of these boats, a rusting fishing trawler in Alaskan waters, because it posed such a serious hazard to shipping.

Invasive species

US scientists are concerned about invasive species of plants and animals that might be carried on wreckage, boats and other debris floating across the Pacific Ocean from Japan. Scientists were surprised that so many creatures survived for more than a year at sea. They collected 1.4 tonnes of marine life from a Japanese dock found beached on the Oregon coast. They also found fish from Japanese waters that had survived *inside* a ship that spent two years floating across the Pacific after the tsunami.

The emergency services react

Emergency service workers were desperate to help people in distress. However, in the worst-hit towns they were unable to do much because their vehicles and other equipment were swept away by the tsunami. Help came from nearby towns, other parts of Japan and also from other countries. It took time to reach the worst-hit towns, because roads and railway tracks were blocked or swept away, and ports and airports were unusable.

About 100,000 members of the Japan Self-Defense Forces were sent to help with the search and rescue work. Japanese air force jets flew **reconnaissance** missions over the affected area to provide information about the situation on the ground. Dozens of ships patrolled the coast looking for victims in the water. Police forces across Japan and the health ministry sent medical and rescue teams. The Japanese Red Cross sent out 115 disaster response teams. Dozens of other countries donated money, sent relief supplies and offered help. The US Navy sent an aircraft carrier with supplies and personnel. Teams of search dogs arrived from the United States and Australia. Japan and China had been experiencing strained relations, but both countries put their differences aside and Japan accepted help from China. Many of the same international emergency workers had helped after the Indonesian tsunami in 2004.

Search teams used dogs because a dog's sense of smell is a thousand times more sensitive than that of humans. The dogs were able to smell people trapped under the debris.

Volunteers collected personal possessions from the rubble. They were cleaned and stored in halls where people could reclaim them.

Searching the rubble

Police officers, soldiers, firefighters and other emergency workers worked long hours searching for people in collapsed buildings and under rubble. They hoped to find live victims but all too often they found only bodies. On the rare occasion when they did find someone alive, it lifted their spirits.

Keeping calm

"There is no sense of panic. People don't shout 'Help!', they ask, 'Please assist me'."

First Lieutenant Hideo Amagai, Japanese Self-Defense Force

Reuniting families

People were often unable to let relatives know they were alive because the telephone network failed. Some families discovered that relatives were alive in strange ways. A Japanese student in California, USA, feared that his family had died in a coastal village until he spotted his sister in a YouTube video holding up a sign saying, "We all survived". A US teacher walked for 20 hours along closed roads and through tsunami debris searching for his girlfriend. Amazingly he found her alive and unhurt.

Dealing with the dead

Search and rescue workers recovered thousands of bodies from the debris. They couldn't search the evacuation zone around the Fukushima Daiichi nuclear power station because of the radiation hazard. Hundreds of bodies were washed up along the coast because the tsunami swept many people out to sea and carried some back to shore with incoming tides. The bodies had to be dealt with quickly to avoid disease.

Identification

Wherever possible, search and rescue workers laid out bodies in makeshift **morgues** set up in local halls. Families visited to try to identify relatives. The process was made more difficult because the tsunami destroyed many of the medical and dental records that usually help in identification. **Deoxyribonucleic acid (DNA)** was taken from every single body. More than 5,000 people were identified by their DNA, but a year after the tsunami, hundreds of bodies remained unidentified.

The teams who performed the grim task of recovering bodies had to work quickly while also treating each body with respect.

Mistaken identity

Police and medical teams were anxious to return bodies to families without delay, but occasionally mistakes were made. Nine bodies are known to have been returned to the wrong families. The families had positively identified photographs of the bodies as those of relatives. However, they were mistaken. The errors came to light when the real families of the dead recognized the photographs and came forward to claim the bodies. DNA tests settled the matter.

Mass burials

In Japan, 99.9 per cent of bodies are usually cremated, but there were so many thousands of bodies that morgues and **crematoria** couldn't cope. Instead, families were urged to agree to **mass burials**, and to exhume the bodies at a later date for cremation. Families did reluctantly agree, but some are reported to have taken bodies away to cremate them themselves.

A six-year-old girl visits her father's grave at a mass burial site in Higashi-Matsushima.

Amazing survival stories

Some people survived by an extraordinary stroke of luck while everyone around them died. When the water receded, it carried debris, cars, even whole buildings, and thousands of people back out to sea. The Japan Maritime Self-Defense Force spotted one man, Hiromitsu Shinkawa, two days after the tsunami. He was 16 kilometres (10 miles) out to sea, floating on the remains of his roof. He'd seen the tsunami approaching and ran into his house to collect some belongings. The tsunami hit the house and swept it, and him, out to sea.

Terrifying sight

"I saw the bottom of the sea when the tidal wave withdrew and houses and people were being washed out. I couldn't watch any more."

A resident of Minamisanriku

Searchers at sea hoped to find people clinging to floating debris. They found one man on his roof, and then a dog that survived for three weeks on a floating house!

A four-month-old baby, swept away and presumed dead, was found alive and unharmed in the rubble three days later. On the same day in the coastal town of Minamisanriku, 42 people were found alive in the wreckage of the devastated town.

Think about this: being a disaster manager

A tsunami has struck a nearby coast and you are the official tasked with handling the disaster in your area. Electrical power has failed. Roads are blocked. Low ground is flooded. Thousands of people are homeless. Some may be trapped in the wreckage of their homes, schools and work-places. News reaches you that fires have broken out in damaged buildings. What do you do first? What are your priorities?

The most urgent task is to save life, so you'll have to get help to people who are trapped or injured. Will local emergency workers be able to cope, or will you have to ask for help from other areas or from national organizations like the army? Once the most urgent tasks are in hand, what will you do next? What help will homeless people need – food, warmth, bedding? Where will these supplies come from? What transport will they need? Can charities help? Can you mobilize volunteers to help? Will it be possible to restore power? Is the water supply safe to drink? If it isn't, what will you do?

Oh, and there are reporters waiting outside for a statement. What will you tell them? Remember, you can use them to get information out to survivors.

You're in the hot seat. It's your decision.

Telling the world

The 2011 Japanese tsunami was a global news story and probably the most intensely filmed and photographed natural disaster in history. The first widespread reports of the disaster were made by ordinary people, not professional reporters, using social media networks.

In the aftermath of the tsunami, the telephone networks failed in some places because of physical damage or because they were overloaded with calls. However, internet-based services such as Skype, Twitter, YouTube and Facebook carried on working. Thousands of people uploaded photographs and videos of the tsunami. Hundreds of thousands of people saw them and then broadcasters picked them up and re-broadcast them to millions more viewers.

North Carolina State University, USA, studied how people used Twitter following the nuclear emergency. They found that it didn't help people share information they wouldn't have found anyway from traditional sources like television, radio and newspapers, but it enabled them to share the information faster than ever.

Appealing for help

Katsunobu Sakurai, the mayor of Minamisoma, a town near the Fukushima Daiichi nuclear power station, used YouTube in an extraordinary way. While other towns waited for help to arrive, he took a different view. He made a video asking for help and pleading with the **media** to come in and witness the situation for themselves. He said, "Until now, we waited for the mass media to come here and videotape us. This time, we reversed the process by taking our video and broadcasting it." As a result, the town received thousands of boxes of food and other supplies from all over the world, and lorryloads of goods from relief organizations.

Fact and fiction

On 19 February 2011, a film called *Hereafter*, directed by Clint Eastwood and starring Matt Damon, was released in Japan. It included scenes depicting the 2004 Asian tsunami. Less than a month after the film's premiere, the Japanese tsunami struck. A few days later, Warner Bros. withdrew the film from all Japanese cinemas, because its terrifying tsunami scenes would be upsetting for many people affected by the disaster.

Web help

The International Red Cross, one of the world's biggest aid organizations, operates a website called Family Links for locating people and reuniting families after a disaster. People can register their details on the site to let families know they are safe, while people looking for relatives can post details of missing persons. After the tsunami, Family Links was overwhelmed. Google helped by launching a similar service. It also set up an account where people could post photographs of the lists of names of people in emergency shelters.

Mayor Katsunobu Sakurai used YouTube to appeal for help for his devastated town.

Tsunamis pictured

When a tsunami struck Hawaii in 1946, a handful of grainy black and white photographs and several films recorded the event. When the Indian Ocean tsunami, the most deadly in recorded history, struck in 2004, tourists captured images of the wave sweeping ashore. When the tsunami hit Japan in 2011, thousands of cameras on the coast, in the towns and in aircraft were trained on the unfolding disaster. As a result, we have moment-by-moment photographs and videos of the tsunami. They form the most complete photographic record of any tsunami in history.

Japan's national TV networks cancelled their programmes and covered the unfolding disaster live. Their output was taken by other broadcasters around the world. There was professionally shot video from camera crews on the ground and in aircraft, and lots of amateur video and pictures shot using mobile phones and digital cameras from witnesses.

Within hours, newspaper readers all over the world were reading headlines like "Horror in Japan" (*Chicago Sun-Times*), "Shock Wave" (*Daily Telegraph*, Australia), "Sea Ravages Japan" (*Asian Age*) and "Tsunami terror slams Japan" (*Indian Express*).

Tourists run from the sea at Hat Rai Lay beach in Thailand as a foaming tsunami wave approaches the coast in 2004.

A cameraman's story

When the tsunami struck Japan in 2011, UK television news cameraman Stuart Webb was packed and ready to go to Libya to cover a revolution happening there. Minutes before he was due to leave for the airport, his editor rang and told him to go to Japan instead and cover the tsunami. He had 10 minutes to repack for Japan in winter instead of the blistering heat of Libya. He also selected different camera gear. He chose his best professional equipment instead of small handheld cameras and helmet-cams that could be used without attracting attention when filming on city streets during a revolution.

He expected he'd find nothing working in the tsunami-hit area, so he packed a satellite phone, military food ration packs and a sleeping bag. After two days travelling by plane, train and car, he reached Minamisanriku, one of the worst-hit towns. While Webb filmed the devastation, the news reporter travelling with him described the eerie silence as searchers retrieved bodies from the wreckage that was once a thriving town. From time to time, they had to leave when further tsunami warnings sounded.

News media cover a visit by Natori City mayor, Isoo Sasaki (in blue), to the tsunami-hit coast.

Press criticism

A survey in Japan in 2011 found that most people were happy with press coverage of the earthquake, but most were unhappy with the way the nuclear emergency was covered.

Japan's newspapers (and television channels) were criticized for merely repeating information issued by the government and the Tokyo Electric Power Company (TEPCO) about the crisis at the Fukushima Daiichi nuclear power station and not asking more searching questions. The official statements were later found to have repeatedly minimized the extent and severity of the disaster. Yasuo Onuki, a Japanese journalist and former executive producer at broadcaster NHK, said, "Rather than trying to find out the truth, the media became a **PR** machine for the establishment."

A different perspective

Some Japanese journalists had a different perspective on the situation. They rejected this criticism. They pointed out that they were trying to report on the biggest peacetime crisis faced by any developed nation while they, too, were victims of it. There was no fuel for their vehicles. Supplies of everything, even paper and ink, were disrupted. Some of the reporters and photographers, even those used to covering foreign wars and conflicts, were traumatized by finding the same distressing sights in their own country affecting their own people.

Reuters is the world's biggest independent international news agency. Wherever something newsworthy is happening, anywhere in the world, you'll find a Reuters journalist. Reuters sells its news stories to newspapers, magazines, broadcasters and other organizations that can't have their own correspondents and photographers in every news hot spot around the world.

The agency has been covering events around the world for more than 160 years. It became successful by being faster than other news organizations. Paul Julius Reuter founded the company in Aachen, Germany, in the 19th century. He famously used carrier pigeons and **telegraph** messages to distribute stock market prices before his rivals. He later extended his service to London, from where he transmitted news to Paris by telegraph. Wherever new telegraph cables were laid, Reuters opened new offices.

QUICK FACTS

FOUNDED:	1851
NUMBER OF JOURNALISTS:	more than 3,000
NUMBER OF NEWS BUREAUS:	200
NUMBER OF NEWS STORIES PRODUCED EVERY YEAR:	2.3 million
NUMBER OF PHOTOGRAPHS AND OTHER IMAGES PRODUCED EACH YEAR:	500,000
NUMBER OF VIDEO STORIES PRODUCED EVERY YEAR:	97,000

Baron Paul Julius Reuter founded Reuters news agency in 1851. He had worked for an even older news agency, Agence France Presse, which also still exists today.

3

Scientists at work

Scientists had a completely different perspective on the disaster from either victims or emergency workers. Scientists focused on gathering data from the disaster. They collected more data from the 2011 Japanese tsunami than from any other natural disaster in history. They started work on it the moment it began, and they will be studying it for years to come. A wide range of different types of scientists work on tsunami research, including **geologists**, **geophysicists**, **seismologists** and **oceanographers**.

Within seconds of the earthquake, scientists saw automatic warnings flash up on computer screens in earthquake and tsunami warning centres around the world. The warnings indicated an earthquake of immense power. The scientists knew Japan had never experienced such a powerful earthquake before and most of them didn't think the fault to the north-east of Japan could possibly produce such a big earthquake, so they literally didn't believe what they were seeing on their computer screens. They expected the fault to produce earthquakes up to about magnitude 8.0 at the most, and to generate tsunamis as high as 2–3 metres (6–10 feet) at Sendai. Their prediction was based on historical records of earthquakes and tsunamis in the region going back a thousand years.

Reporters are briefed on the 2011 Japanese tsunami at the French tsunami warning centre near Paris.

Making predictions

Scientists often disagree with each other, propose conflicting theories and make different predictions for the future. While most scientists were surprised by the 2011 earthquake and tsunami, at least one scientist did predict it. In 2006, Yasutaka Ikeda, a seismologist from the University of Tokyo, said that if the fault off north-east Japan's coast ever released all of the stress it had built up over the last century instead of just some of it, as most scientists expected, it could produce a gigantic earthquake. He didn't expect it to happen during his lifetime, but on 11 March 2011 his theory was proved correct.

As more information arrived at tsunami warning centres, it became clear that the 11 March earthquake was indeed far more powerful than the magnitude 8.0 most scientists expected. Scientists realized that this quake could produce an enormous tsunami, far worse than anyone had planned for, and they started warning authorities in the area.

Warning sounds

Scientists working in areas that seem totally unconnected with tsunamis sometimes find themselves contributing to tsunami research. For example, after the 2004 Asian tsunami, scientists who normally analyse underwater sounds for evidence of nuclear weapons tests discovered that the tsunami produced a unique sound signal. In the future, this discovery might be used as part of a worldwide tsunami warning system.

Analysing the data

Seismologists and geologists analysed all the available data. They viewed all the photographs and video, especially video of the tsunami shot from the air, which showed the water sweeping across farmland. This had never been seen so clearly before.

Scientists study tsunamis and check their theories and predictions by programming computers to show how tsunamis behave. These simulations are called computer models. Diana Greenslade, Principal Research Scientist, Australian Bureau of **Meteorology**, said, "The amount of video, especially from the helicopter where you can actually see the wave front inundating onto the land, is exactly what we need to be able to verify our [computer] models".

Scientists arrive

Scientists from around the world arrived in Japan within days of the tsunami to study the disaster at first hand. They looked for evidence of the tsunami's height and how far it travelled inland. They could see that the tsunami had been much higher in some places than others.

Improving models

When the Indian Ocean basin suffered the deadliest tsunami in 2004, computer models showing how tsunamis spread across the ocean were very basic. There were also very few tsunami sensors in the Indian Ocean since it was thought that large tsunamis would be unlikely to occur there. Then it wasn't possible to predict where a tsunami would travel to and which countries were at risk straight after the earthquake. Now it is.

Just a few years ago, countries as far away as Australia would have had to issue tsunami warnings and evacuate exposed coastlines. This time, Australian scientists could see straight away that their computer models predicted no impact for Australia, so no warnings or evacuations were needed. And data from the 2011 Japanese tsunami will further improve these computer models, and make future tsunami warnings more accurate and reliable. This is important, because if people are repeatedly warned of tsunamis that don't arrive or aren't as bad as predicted, there is a risk that they will stop listening to the warnings.

Tsunami satellites

Some Earth-monitoring satellites carry instruments that measure the sea level to within a few centimetres, so they're able to detect tsunamis moving across the ocean. Three satellites spotted the Japanese tsunami – NASA/**Centre National d'Études Spatiales's (CNES)** Jason 1, NASA/European Jason 2 and the **European Space Agency's (ESA)** Envisat.

Double tsunami

When scientists analysed data from satellites passing over Japan on 11 March 2011, they discovered that this was a unique type of tsunami. In fact, two tsunami waves created by the earthquake merged together to form an even bigger tsunami. This is the first time this has ever been seen, although scientists think it may have happened before in 1960 when a massive earthquake off the coast of Chile sent a tsunami racing across the Pacific Ocean. Tony Song, a scientist at the **National Aeronautics and Space Administration (NASA)** Jet Propulsion Laboratory in California, USA, said, "It was a 1 in 10 million chance that we were able to observe this double wave with satellites."

Scientists who visited Japan after the disaster estimated the height of the tsunami in various places by looking for evidence, including cars and boats that had been lifted onto the roofs of buildings.

Health checks

Doctors and scientists will be monitoring the health of tsunami victims for years to come. Children's health will be monitored very closely, because they are the ones who are most at risk from radioactive iodine, which can cause **thyroid** cancer. Several thousand cases of thyroid cancer in children and teenagers were reported after the Chernobyl nuclear accident in 1986. More than 100 children in the Fukushima region were checked in October 2011. They will be checked again every two years until the age of 20, and then every five years.

Food monitoring

Scientists carried out extensive tests on people and crops in the area to check for radioactive contamination. Fukushima city gave 34,000 special instruments called radiation dosimeters to children, who wore them for three months to collect information about their exposure to radiation. Farm crops were tested weekly. Food testing will continue in Japan for decades. Ukraine and Belarus still monitor food for radiation more than 25 years after the Chernobyl nuclear accident.

The Japanese government said the tests made sure that no tainted food could reach the shops. However, the public became concerned when contaminated tea leaves and beef were found to be on sale. Then a health ministry official said it was impossible to eliminate contaminated products from sale completely because it was impossible to test every product.

Why is radiation dangerous?

Nuclear radiation can damage DNA, the **genetic code** inside living cells. This can cause cancer or birth defects in babies. However, radiation is safe while it is sealed inside a nuclear reactor. The damage caused by the tsunami at the Fukushima Daiichi power station allowed harmful amounts of radiation to escape into the environment. Two months later, scientists found butterflies nearby suffering from genetic damage caused by radiation.

Tracking fish

Bluefin tuna caught near California, USA, several months after the tsunami were found to contain radioactive particles from Fukushima. Scientists plan to use this discovery to track the unknown migration routes of these fish.

The human guinea pig

Nobuyoshi Ito was the manager of an agricultural research centre in the village of Iitate. The village is just outside the nuclear exclusion zone round the Fukushima Daiichi nuclear power station, but it was evacuated because it was found to be a **radiation hot spot**. The 68-year-old Ito was one of a handful of the 6,200 residents who refused to leave. His presence in the town proved to be very useful. Samples of rice he collected from **paddy fields** were tested and found to be within safe radiation limits.

A young girl is checked for radiation exposure at an evacuation centre in Nihonmatsu, Fukushima prefecture.

Health impact

So far, the main health effect of the tsunami and nuclear accident on survivors appears to be psychological. Many of the thousands of people who suffered the loss of friends and family may find it hard to shake off upsetting thoughts and memories. Tatsuya Suzuki, who lived in Yuriage, a fishing port, said, "Even though one year has passed, nothing has really changed. Time has stopped for me ... For others, the disaster may be becoming a thing of the past, but for us, it is still our reality today. I think we are still grieving."

Some victims cope better than others. Chihiro Kanno, a young resident of Rikuzentakata, said, "When I am alone I cannot help thinking about my friends who died. I really long to see them again. But when I am with my friends I am fine."

Delayed effects

Victims who witnessed the worst scenes and suffered the most severe losses are at risk of developing a serious psychological condition called post traumatic stress disorder. Sufferers may experience flashbacks (upsetting memories), insomnia (an inability to sleep) or feelings of guilt that they survived while others died. It can take months or even years to develop.

Feelings of grief, loss and despair were common among tsunami survivors. More serious psychological problems may not emerge for years.

Long-term problems

According to World Health Organization (WHO) researchers, the numbers of people suffering from psychological problems can double after a disaster, although only a small percentage need treatment. After the Indonesian tsunami in 2004, WHO estimated that 50 per cent of those affected might experience psychological problems such as stress, grief, anxiety and depression, with 5–10 per cent having more serious problems that require treatment. The Indonesian government responded with the country's biggest ever mental health programme. Japan's triple disaster (earthquake, tsunami and nuclear accident) will no doubt lead to long-term mental health problems, which will require careful monitoring and, in some cases, treatment.

Environmental impact

For the first time, National Aeronautics and Space Administration (NASA) scientists observed icebergs '**calving**' (breaking away from an ice shelf) as a result of a tsunami. The 2011 Japanese tsunami took 18 hours to travel 13,600 km (8,500 mi.) to Antarctica, where it broke up part of the Sulzberger Ice Shelf. Satellite photographs showed chunks of ice twice the size of Manhattan, New York City, breaking off and drifting away.

Members of the Japan Ladies Professional Golf Association collected money to help tsunami victims.

Recovery and reconstruction

The earthquake and tsunami created more than 180 million tonnes of debris. It had to be cleared away before rebuilding could begin. Thousands of **excavators** and other heavy machinery were needed. One manufacturer, Komatsu, estimated that 5,000 of its machines were in use in the tsunami-hit area. Japan's construction machinery industry saw an increase of 42 per cent in orders for heavy machinery after the tsunami. The priority was to clear roads so that search, rescue and recovery vehicles could get through.

Danger in the air

The government wanted the debris left behind by the tsunami cleared as fast as possible. There was no shortage of volunteers willing to do the work, but the debris was dangerous. It released hazardous dust and fibres containing cancer-causing asbestos and dioxins. Workers clearing it had to wear face masks while officials monitored the levels of dust and fibres in the air. Tetsuo Ishii, a Sendai city official, said, "The biggest concerns are dirt, sand and building dust that can be inhaled and cause abnormalities in the lungs."

An excavator clears tsunami debris in Rikuzentakata.

Temporary houses like this complex in Rikuzentakata sprang up throughout northeast Japan.

Land pollution

A lot of the contamination caused by the tsunami couldn't be cleared up, because it was made up of seawater, oil and other liquids that soaked into the ground, polluting farmland. The Tōhoku region grew more than a quarter of Japan's rice crop. Kanto, another region affected by the tsunami, accounted for another 19 per cent. The tsunami will affect farm production in Japan for decades to come, requiring Japan to import more of its food.

Housing the homeless

After the disaster, more than 500,000 people were living in temporary shelters. They all had to be supplied with food and water. Most of them only had the clothes they were wearing. It was a daunting situation for officials to have to deal with. Tens of thousands of people were stranded in the worst-hit areas as search and rescue workers tried to get to them. In addition, thousands of people were evacuated from the Fukushima area because of the nuclear accident there. Tens of thousands of temporary and **prefabricated homes** had to be built quickly to house the homeless.

Tough times

"In the 65 years since the end of World War II, this is the toughest and the most difficult crisis for Japan."

Naoto Kan, Japanese Prime Minister at the time of the tsunami

43

Nuclear clean-up

Workers will be cleaning up the Fukushima Daiichi nuclear power station for decades to come, perhaps 40 years. The clean-up is being monitored by scientists from the International Atomic Energy Agency (IAEA). The work is difficult, because the workers have to wear bulky protective suits and suffocating face masks. An un-named clean-up worker at the Fukushima Daiichi nuclear power station said, "Underneath your suit and mask, you're drenched with sweat." Despite the risks and discomfort, unemployed people from all over Japan travelled to the power plant looking for work.

The next tsunami

One earthquake can often trigger earthquakes in nearby faults. Scientists are now watching a fault to the south of Japan very closely in case it suddenly gives way, perhaps setting off another destructive tsunami on Japan's southern coast. It could happen tomorrow or it might not happen for decades.

Nuclear fuel that hadn't melted began to be removed in November 2013 when Fukushima Daiichi's nuclear reactors had cooled down. After about 10 years, melted fuel will be removed. Then the buildings will be dismantled. Meanwhile, radioactive fall-out on the surrounding land is being dealt with. Buildings were washed down to clean off radioactive particles. Contaminated soil was scraped off the ground and taken away to be stored safely. A large area of seabed near the power station was sealed with 60 centimetres (2 feet) of cement to stop radioactive fall-out in the mud spreading further out to sea.

A worker monitors the radiation level at the damaged Fukushima Daiichi nuclear power station.

Anti-nuclear protests persuaded the Japanese government to change its nuclear policy and begin shutting down the country's nuclear reactors.

Continuing problems

In 2013, two years after the emergency, the damaged reactors were still unstable and still having to be cooled by pumping seawater into them. The water is being stored until it can be decontaminated. It was later discovered that some of the hundreds of water storage tanks built at the plant were leaking radioactive water.

Changing attitudes to nuclear power

Until the 2011 tsunami, the Japanese government and most of the Japanese people were in favour of nuclear power. However, after the tsunami and nuclear accident, there was such a surge in opposition to nuclear power that the government began shutting down the country's nuclear reactors. Most were shut down by 5 May 2012, although a few have been restarted since then to prevent electricity blackouts.

Government criticism

The Japanese people are renowned for their calmness and dignity in adversity, but some criticized the government for being too slow to help them. The Prime Minister, Naoto Kan, was said to be indecisive. He resigned five months after the tsunami.

Rebuilding

Rebuilding after a tsunami is a slow process. Two years after the Asian tsunami in 2004, 25,000 families in Banda Aceh in Indonesia were still homeless. Millions of dollars poured into the region, but less than half of the homes needed had been built. Five years after the tsunami, 1,300 families in Sri Lanka were still in temporary housing.

Reconstruction of the Tōhoku region devastated by the Japanese tsunami in 2011 is expected to take 10 years. But in 2013, two years after the tsunami, very little rebuilding had started. People blame government **red tape**, a lack of urgency and poor coordination between the government and local authorities. There were reports that developers couldn't get permission to build on land that had been farmland before the tsunami but was now so contaminated that farming was no longer allowed on it. Local officials wouldn't allow it to be built on because it hadn't been officially "re-zoned" from agricultural land to residential land.

Business and industry

Business and industry had to be rebuilt, too. The fishing industry was very badly affected. More than 20,000 fishing boats were damaged, sunk or swept away. Instead of waiting for government compensation to arrive, the fishermen in one town, Ogatsu, took matters into their own hands. They sold shares for 10,000 yen (£63) each to private investors. By the end of 2011, they had sold 20,000 shares. Their aim is to sell 50,000. The money they raise will be used to buy new boats and equipment. Hiromi Ito, a fisherman in Ogatsu, said, "I looked at the devastation and decided there and then that we had to build a new kind of business run by fishermen, for fishermen."

Most of Ogatsu's residents survived the tsunami, but thousands left the town to live on safer, higher ground further inland. There are so few people left in some of the smaller coastal towns that they may never be rebuilt.

Home comforts

"What I really want is to once again have 'my home'."

Migaku Suzuki, a citizen of Rikuzentakata

If you lived in a town that was destroyed by a tsunami, would you be happy to return to the coast and live there again? What would be the arguments for and against doing this? If you were to move back to a coastal town, how do you think it might be made safer when the next tsunami happens?

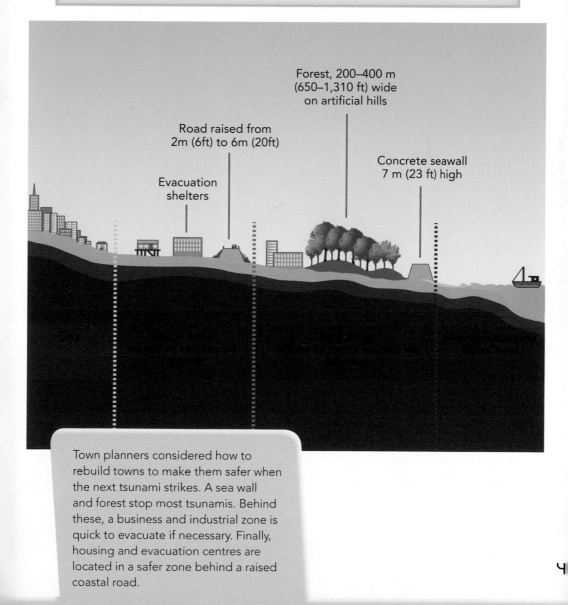

Forest, 200–400 m
(650–1,310 ft) wide
on artificial hills

Road raised from
2m (6ft) to 6m (20ft)

Concrete seawall
7 m (23 ft) high

Evacuation
shelters

Town planners considered how to rebuild towns to make them safer when the next tsunami strikes. A sea wall and forest stop most tsunamis. Behind these, a business and industrial zone is quick to evacuate if necessary. Finally, housing and evacuation centres are located in a safer zone behind a raised coastal road.

What have we learned?

Every disaster has lessons that can be learned and used when dealing with future disasters. Here are some of the lessons learned from the 2011 Japanese tsunami:

- Natural disasters like tsunamis can surprise experts by happening at an unexpected time or in an unexpected place.
- A tsunami can overwhelm even the most economically advanced and well-prepared nations, like Japan.
- A tsunami can be much more destructive than the earthquake that caused it.
- Tsunami drills save lives by showing people what they must do if a tsunami warning sounds.
- Nuclear accidents, including those caused by natural disasters, are so dangerous and so long-lasting, perhaps affecting generations yet to be born, that nuclear power station builders and operators must plan for the worst possible case, however rare and unexpected it might be.
- It is unwise to build multiple nuclear reactors close together, because a disaster that damages one is likely to affect others nearby, too.
- Homeless victims need special help to resume normal lives without delay. Governments may have to abandon or adapt their usual ways of working, which are often too slow and bureaucratic for dealing with disasters.

Planning for disaster

A natural disaster such as a tsunami can cause great loss of life, damage, disruption and chaos, and these have to be dealt with. It is useful to have a plan so that the disaster can be managed as quickly and efficiently as possible. Tsunamis and other natural disasters are dealt with in two stages: the emergency response stage and the recovery stage. The emergency response stage usually lasts for a few weeks at most, when disaster managers take the most urgent actions necessary to preserve life. They can then move on to the recovery stage. This may last for several years, when the affected area is returned to normal by clearing debris and rebuilding.

A message from the emperor

"I pray that the peaceful lives of those affected can resume as soon as possible."

Emperor Akihito of Japan

Tsunami

Assess the situation

Evacuation

Emergency response

Search and rescue

Emergency medical care

Food and water supplies

Clear debris

Recovery

Long-term health and psychological care

Restore power and water

Rebuild houses and other buildings

Restore roads and transport

A disaster web maps the actions necessary to deal with a disaster such as a tsunami.

Timeline

A timeline of events of the tsunami and its aftermath

2011 11 March	At 2.46 p.m. local time, a magnitude 9.0 earthquake occurs close to the north-east coast of Japan. Buildings shake violently as far away as Tokyo, hundreds of kilometres from the epicentre.
	Electrical power fails at the Fukushima Daiichi nuclear power station. Back-up generators take over.
	A 14-metre (46-foot) high tsunami wave sweeps over the power station and puts its back-up generators out of action
	A fire breaks out at the Cosmo oil refinery in Ichihara near Tokyo
	Coastal areas of Hawaii are evacuated
	In the evening, a nuclear emergency is declared by the government
	The first casualty reports arrive – 32 dead
	Residents living within 2 kilometres (1.2 miles) of the Fukushima Daiichi nuclear power station are evacuated
	Within half an hour, the evacuation order is extended to 3 kilometres (1.9 miles)
	A dam in Fukushima breaks, sending water through a residential area
	The four nuclear power stations closest to the earthquake epicentre are shut down
12 March	At the Fukushima Daiichi nuclear power station, steam is released from one of the reactors to reduce the pressure inside
	The evacuation order is extended to 10 kilometres (6 miles)
	An explosion rips one of the reactor buildings apart
	The government mobilizes 100,000 military and other staff to help with the relief effort
	The Fukushima evacuation order is extended to 20 kilometres (12 miles)
13 March	Estimates of the death toll rise steeply to more than 10,000
	A man is rescued at sea, floating on the roof of his house
	Electricity rationing begins as a result of nuclear power station shut-downs

14 March	Searchers find 2,000 bodies in Miyagi prefecture A reactor building at the Fukushima Daiichi nuclear power station explodes
15 March	There are further explosions at the Fukushima Daiichi nuclear power station Officials distribute iodine tablets at evacuation centres to protect people from radiation
May	73,000 homes are still without water and 10,500 have no electricity
August	Most of the debris is removed from residential areas
September	The Tohoku Shinkansen (Bullet Train) service returns to normal operation
2012	A National Reconstruction Agency is set up Sewage treatment plants in the affected area return to normal operation Twelve districts announce plans to raise the ground level by up to 17 metres (55 feet) before rebuilding towns in the same locations Debris from the tsunami begins to wash up on the west coasts of Canada and the United States
2013	Removal of unmelted fuel from the Fukushima Daiichi nuclear power station begins
2015	Major fishing ports should be restored to working order
2021	Removal of melted fuel from the Fukushima Daiichi nuclear power station will begin
2030–2040	Dismantling of the Fukushima Daiichi nuclear power station should be completed

Glossary

asteroid rocky or metallic natural object in orbit around the Sun; also called a minor planet

avalanche fast flow of a large amount of land, snow or ice down a mountainside

Buddhist someone who believes in a religion called Buddhism

buoy large floating object anchored to keep it in one place, to mark the position of something, to warn of danger or to collect information

bureaucracy a system of government by strictly following a fixed procedure which often results in delay

calving in the case of ice, the break-up of the edge of an ice sheet or glacier, which produces icebergs

Centre National d'Études Spatiales (CNES) French government's space agency

comet object made of rock, dust and ice that orbits the Sun

condolence money money traditionally given in Japan by friends and relatives when a family member dies

crematoria buildings where bodies are disposed of by burning

crust rocky surface layer of Earth or another planet or moon

debris accumulation of fragments of rock, rubbish, or pieces of something broken or destroyed

deoxyribonucleic acid (DNA) substance inside a living cell that contains an organism's genetic code

dosimeter device for measuring exposure to radiation

epicentre point on Earth's surface directly above the place where an earthquake occurs underground

European Space Agency (ESA) intergovernmental organization dedicated to exploring space, with 20 member states from Europe

excavator digging machine

fall-out radioactive particles released into the environment by a nuclear accident or explosion

fault line where two or more tectonic plates meet; where earthquakes are likely to occur

genetic code instructions in the DNA inside an organism's cells that control the organism's growth and development

geologist scientist who studies Earth's rocks and minerals, and how they were formed

geophysicist scientist who studies the physics of Earth, its atmosphere, its oceans and the space surrounding it

mantle rock inside Earth – or another planet or moon – between the core and the crust

mass burial burying a large number of bodies in the same grave

media term used to describe radio, television, newspapers, magazines and the internet

meltdown in a nuclear reactor, overheating of the fuel to a temperature high enough to melt it

meteorology scientific study of the atmosphere and weather

morgue place where bodies are kept until they are identified, autopsied or released for burial. A morgue in a funeral home or hospital is also called a mortuary.

National Aeronautics and Space Administration (NASA) US space and flight research agency

nuclear fuel radioactive substance such as uranium or plutonium that is used to produce heat inside a nuclear power station, to boil water and produce steam to drive electricity generators

nuclear reactor device in which nuclear energy is released from a fuel, such as uranium. In a nuclear power station, the energy heats water to make steam which is used to drive a generator to make electricity. A nuclear power station may have several reactors.

oceanographer scientist who studies Earth's oceans, including their biology, chemistry and geology

paddy field flooded piece of farmland where rice is grown

PR public relations: providing information about an organisation to the public so that people will regard that organisation in a favourable way

prefabricated home building manufactured, sometimes in sections, in a factory and then transported to the place where people will live in it

prefecture 1 of 47 administrative regions within Japan, similar to counties in the UK and states in the United States

radiation energy and particles given out by something. Nuclear radiation is dangerous to living organisms and so nuclear reactors are heavily shielded.

radiation hot spot place where the radiation level is higher than in the surrounding area

radioactive giving out nuclear radiation

reconnaissance visiting or exploring an area to gather information about it

red tape unnecessary or overcomplicated rules

reservoir natural or man-made lake that is used for storing water

seismologist scientist who studies earthquakes

subduction process in which one plate of Earth's crust pushes under the edge of another plate

tectonic plate piece of Earth's crust that covers Earth like a cracked eggshell

telegraph device for sending simple messages over long distances by using electric impulses travelling along wires

thyroid one of several parts of the body called glands that release substances into the body to control its growth, use of energy and chemical activity. The thyroid gland is in the neck.

Find out more

Non-fiction books

Disaster Relief, Nick Hunter (Raintree, 2012)

Disasters (Discover More), David Burnie (Scholastic Reference, 2013)

Earthquakes and Tsunamis, Emily Bone (Usborne, 2012)

I Survived the Japanese Tsunami, 2011, Lauren Tarshis (Scholastic, 2013)

Natural Disasters, Claire Watts (Dorling Kindersley, 2012)

Plate Tectonics and Disasters, Tom Greve (Rourke Educational Media, 2012)

Tsunamis (Eyewitness Disaster), Helen Dwyer (Franklin Watts, 2011)

Tsunamis (Natural Disasters), Richard and Louise Spilsbury (Wayland, 2012)

Fiction books

Escaping the Giant Wave, Peg Kehret (Aladdin Paperbacks, 2004)

The Killing Sea, Richard Lewis (Simon & Schuster Children's, 2006)

The Tsunami Countdown, Boyd Morrison (Sphere, 2012)

Films

Earth: The Power of the Planet (2008)

Tsunami – The Killer Wave (2005)

Websites

environment.nationalgeographic.com/environment/natural-disasters/tsunami-safety-tips.html
This website has tsunami safety tips from National Geographic.

news.bbc.co.uk/cbbcnews/hi/newsid_4130000/newsid_4137800/4137839.stm
This is an animated guide to the 2004 Asian tsunami from the BBC.

news.nationalgeographic.com/news/2011/03/110311-tsunami-facts-japan-earthquake-hawaii
This website from National Geographic has lots of tsunami facts.

www.nhm.ac.uk/nature-online/earth/volcanoes-earthquakes/tsunami/index.html

This is an introduction to tsunamis from Britain's Natural History Museum.

www.tsunami.noaa.gov/kids.html

On this website you'll find lots of links for information pages, activities and educational resources about tsunamis from the National Oceanic and Atmospheric Administration (NOAA).

www.tsunami.gov

This website gives details of the latest tsunami warnings from the United States NOAA's National Weather Service.

More topics to research

1. Where are the major seismological faults around the world and which of these faults could produce tsunamis? Remember, not all underwater faults produce tsunamis. Look for subduction zones.
2. Where is the Cascadia subduction zone, and why might this produce a tsunami? Which major cities in North America would be affected by it?
3. Are there any Native American legends about tsunamis?
4. What is The Great Wave off Kanagawa? How old is it and who produced it? Is it a tsunami? If it isn't a tsunami, then what is it?
5. When did a tsunami hit the coast of Portugal?
6. Scientists have found evidence of tsunamis and mega-tsunamis in prehistoric times. What rare event caused a mega-tsunami that occurred 65 million years ago?

Index